AMAZING ASIAN AMERICANS

Amazing Asian Americans

Patsy Mink,
Mother of Title 9

by
Ai-Ling Louie

Illustrated by
H.Rick Pettway

Patsy Mink, Mother of Title 9

To Sean — A.L.

Dedicated to the bravest person I know, my sister Deborah E. Pettway
who is recovering from a successful double lung transplant. All my love. — H.R.P

Copyright ©2018 by Ai-Ling Louie. All rights reserved. No part of this publication may be reproduced, stored in a retrievable system or transmitted in any form or by any means, electronic, mechanical, photocopying, recording or otherwise without the prior written permission of the copyright holder, except brief quotations in a review.

Illustrations ©2018 by H. Rick Pettway

Printed on: Cover, 250 gsm C1S Artcard; Text. IVO 100 gsm Woodfree paper
ISBN 9780978746520
Library of Congress Control # 2017918400
Published by Dragoneagle Press
P.O. Box 30856
Bethesda, Maryland 20824
Dragoneagle.com

Published 2018
First paperback printing 2018

Publisher's Cataloging-in-Publication Data
Louie, Ai-Ling 1949-
    Patsy Mink, Mother of Title 9
        by Ai-Ling Louie
        Illustrations by H.Rick Pettway
        Series: Amazing Asian Americans
        Summary. Juvenile biography of a US Congresswoman,
        the first woman of color elected to Congress, and the co-writer
        of Title IX— which gave equal money to females in
        education and sports.
        ISBN - 9780978746520
        1. Mink, Patsy 1927-2002 - Juvenile Literature
        2. Representatives - United States Congress - Juvenile Literature
        3. Government - United States - Congress - Biography
        4. Asian Americans - Juvenile - LIterature
        5. Japanese Americans - Biography
        6. Women - Biography
        7. Hawai'i - Biography
        8. Sports - Women
        I. Pettway, H.Rick

2018
328.73

Manufactured in Hong Kong by Regal Printing Limited
Last page — painting, "Bamboo Under Spring Rain" c.1460
by Xia Chang, 1388—1470, www.philamuseum.org

Patsy Mink
Mother of Title 9

Amazing Asian Americans

by Ai-Ling Louie
illustrated by H. Rick Pettway

dragoneagle press

Patsy spent many a long summer day happy in the blue waters of the Pacific.

She ended each day playing a friendly baseball game with the neighborhood boys.

When September came, Patsy and her brother Eugene travelled out of their neighborhood to another school. There the Takemoto children were greeted by students calling them names and making fun of the Japanese language.

Patsy went home and complained to her parents who told her, "Ignore those kids, and concentrate on your studies." But Patsy couldn't ignore the constant name-calling. The hurt it caused stayed with her long afterward. She couldn't and wouldn't forget it.

Patsy was a Japanese American girl. Her grandparents came to Maui, one of the Hawaiian islands, to work in the pineapple fields. They stayed and became American citizens. When Patsy was in high school, Japan bombed Pearl Harbor, the Navy base on the Hawaiian island right next to Maui. That was the beginning of World War II for America.

It was a very difficult time for Patsy and all Japanese Americans. The United States wanted to take all Japanese Americans away from the coast and lock them in prison camps so they couldn't spy for Japan. Luckily for Patsy, there was no place in Hawai'i to lock up all the Japanese Americans. The people of California, Oregon, and Washington weren't so lucky.[1] Now, even though there was not a single case of a Japanese American spying, a new name was added to the abuse yelled at Patsy: "Traitor!" She couldn't and wouldn't forget the sting of that horrible lie.

After the war, Patsy went to college at the University of Nebraska. She was her own woman now, living far away from her parents. The university put her in a dorm for foreign students. She told them, "But I'm not foreign. I'm an American just like you." The college insisted, and Patsy knew she was being treated unfairly. This time she wasn't going to ignore the slight. She wrote an angry letter to the school newspaper saying, "Some people do not care if I am of Japanese origin, for they delight in the things I can offer."[2] Patsy talked to a lot of her friends and her teachers too. She got people to come to a big meeting. The university decided to change its rules. Patsy had won her first big fight. She would always remember how good that felt.

Patsy decided she wanted to continue to work
to change things that were unfair. She would make
it her goal in life. She applied to law school to get
the training she needed. The law schools all told her,
"You are an excellent student. Unfortunately we don't
accept women." Well that stung! Finally one law school
said yes. Patsy became a lawyer, but she couldn't
and wouldn't forget being shut out because
she was a woman.

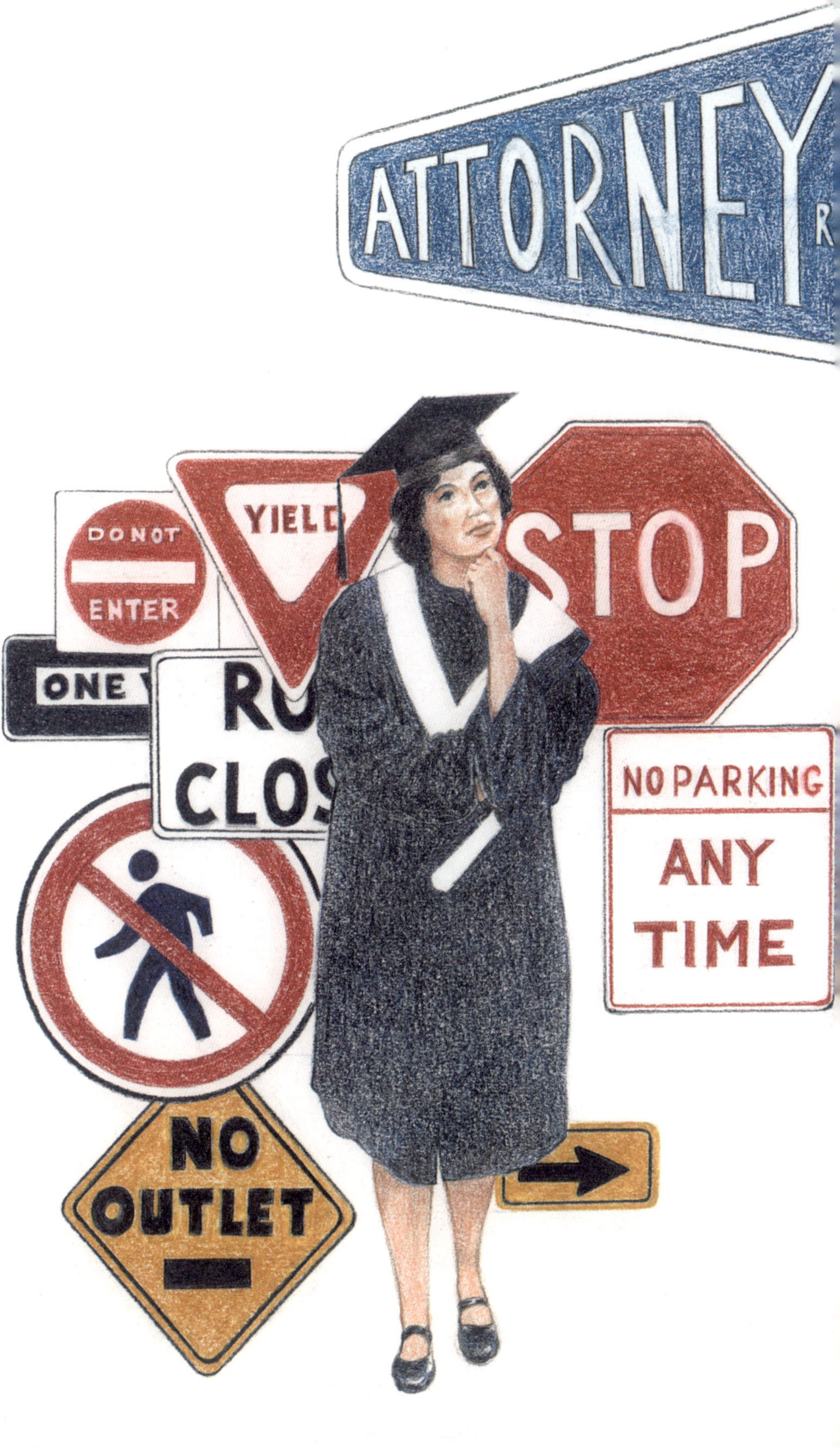

ATTORNEY
DO NOT
ENTER
YIELD
STOP
ONE
NO PARKING
ANY
TIME
NO
OUTLET

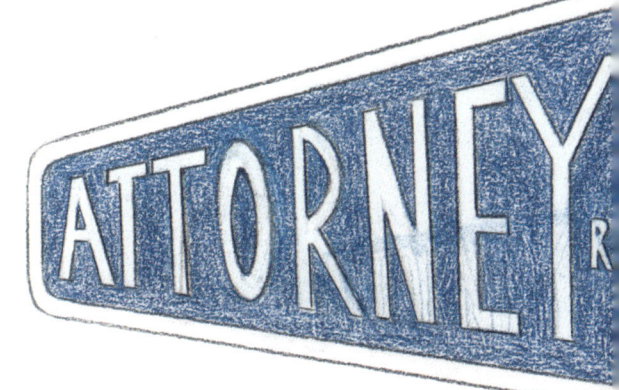

Patsy was denied a job at law firms all across Hawai'i. "You are a wife and mother. Stay home and take care of your child," they told her. But Patsy didn't see it that way. She opened her own law office.

Patsy, her daughter Wendy, and her husband John Mink were on hand to welcome Hawaiʻi into the United States as its 50th state.[3] She was the only woman elected to serve on the state of Hawaiʻi's first governing body.

Patsy had a big dream. She wanted to work
for the good of all Americans, not just Hawaiians.
No other woman of color had ever been elected to serve
in Congress. This did not stop Patsy. She bought a
Daruma doll,[4] to spur her on. She painted in one eye
and promised—if she accomplished her goals—
she would paint in the other.

Many of her days were spent knocking on doors to talk to people and making speeches saying, "I will speak up for everyday people and for children and their schools." In 1965 she won her election and became the first non-white woman ever to serve on Capitol Hill. She was now proud to be known as Representative Patsy T. Mink.

There were 553 men in Congress and only 11 women. There was one other woman on the Education Committee, Edith Green from Oregon. She became Patsy's friend. Patsy said, "Let's put our heads together and see what we can do." Patsy told Edith about how she had been rejected from law school because she was a woman. She said, "I want to do something so that my daughter and your granddaughter don't have to go through that.

Patsy and Edith found a way. They wrote a few simple words that declared that the United States will only give money to schools that treat girls as equals to boys.[5] They put it in an education bill, and it became known as Title 9. It was just 23 little words, but it made such a big difference! Now schools and colleges couldn't and wouldn't say they didn't want women. They had to give them an equal chance at getting a good education.

Those 23 little words that made up Title 9 had some big surprises packed in them. When Patsy and Edith wrote them, they didn't know how much it would change sports. Giving equal treatment to girls' teams in schools and colleges meant that girls began to play soccer, swim, and run with the help of money for coaches, equipment, and scholarships.

Girls' participation in school sports skyrocketed. American girls and women became interested in having healthy and fit bodies. American women's teams began to win more Olympic medals than American men's teams. And it was all due to the fact that Title 9 gave American girls a chance to compete from a young age.[6]

Of course this made many male coaches and athletes jealous. They didn't like having to share sports money and equipment. They got some of their congressmen to write a law weakening Title 9.⁷ Edith Green was no longer a member of Congress. It was up to Patsy Mink to save Title 9.

Patsy fought the fight of her life. She couldn't and wouldn't let Title 9 go down. She gave strong speeches and made a ton of phone calls to other representatives. She went up to them in the halls and poked her finger in their chests and said, "You know very well this law is unfair—it's positively un-American! Do I have your vote?"

Patsy was in charge of the House vote. As she worked the aisles, she was handed a message from her husband. "Wendy in a car accident. Come quickly!"⁸ Patsy ran from the floor, and the vote lost.

Patsy's enemies let it be known that she left crying because she was losing. Her friends knew differently. They arranged a revote. This time Patsy's side won. She had saved Title 9! From this time on, she was known as the "Mother of Title 9." Title 9 is still one of the most far-reaching, important laws of our land.

Patsy Mink served in Congress for 23 years. She died in 2002. She fought for fairness and equality. She couldn't and wouldn't give in. Her fighting spirit and mighty words will live on, bettering all our lives.

And that Daruma doll—it's now seeing into a bright future for girls and boys with both its eyes wide open.

NOTES

[1] Japan bombed Pearl Harbor on December 7, 1941. On the West Coast, 110,000 Japanese Americans were forced into prison camps, such as Manzanar in California. They lost their homes, businesses, pets and schools. In 1988 Congress made an official apology to the Japanese Americans and awarded each survivor $20,000.

[2] Takemoto, Patsy. December 31, 1947, Lincoln, Nebraska, *Daily Nebraskan*.

[3] Hawai'i was a US Territory until August 21, 1959, when it became a state.

[4] A daruma doll is made of papier mâché. The owner paints in one eye to make a promise to do something. She paints in the other eye when the promise is fulfilled.

[5] *US Educational Amendments of 1972, Public Law 92-318, 86. Statute 235*, known as Title 9. "No person in the United States shall, on the basis of sex, be excluded from participation in... any program receiving federal financial assistance."

[6] Myre, Greg. August 21, 2016. *US Women are the Biggest Winners at the Rio Olympics*. NPR, WAMU. "But that same year, (1972) Congress passed Title IX, barring sex discrimination in education programs that receive federal funding. This has helped revolutionize women's sports at both the high school and college levels. American women are now dominant in many sports, including gymnastics, swimming, basketball, rowing, water polo and soccer."

[7] *Tower Amendment*. May 20, 1974, 120 Congressional Record, 15.322-15-323. said that money-making school teams would NOT have to share their income with other teams.

[8] Wendy's accident was serious, but she recovered over the next several months.

TIMELINE

December 6, 1927 born Patsy Takemoto in Paia, Maui, Territory of Hawai'i

1951 graduates from University of Chicago Law School

1956 elected to the Hawai'i Territorial Legislature

August 21, 1959 Hawai'i becomes the 50th State

1962 elected to the Hawai'i State Senate

1965 elected to the United States House of Representatives from Hawai'i's at-large-district. She was the first woman of color to serve in the House or the Senate.

1972 works with Edith Green to write Title IX, an act to amend the Higher Education Act of 1972

1974 is instrumental in defeating attempts to weaken Title IX (Tower Amendment)

August 30, 2002 dies at the age of 75. She served 25 years in the House—12 years, from 1965—1977, and 14 years, from 1989—2002.

SOURCES AND SUGGESTED READING

Bassford, Kimberlee. (2008) *Patsy Mink—Ahead of the Majority*. DVD.

Blumenthal, Karen. (2005) *Let Me Play: The Story of Title IX; The Law that Changed the Future of Girls in America*. New York. Atheneum Books for Young Readers. Grade 7+

Burgan, Michael. (2017) *Japanese American Internment*. North Mankato, MN. Compass Point. Grade 5+.

Calkhoven, Laurie. (2015) *50 Women Who Changed the World*. New York, Scholastic, Juvenile Grade 4—6.

Davidson, Sue. (1994) *A Heart in Politics: Jeanette Rankin and Patsy T. Mink (Women Who Dared)*. Berkeley, CA. Seal Press.

Fremon, David. (2015) *The Internment of Japanese Americans in United States History*. Springfield, NJ. Enslow. Grades 4-6.

Gavora, Jessica. (2002) *Tilting the Playing Field*. New York. Encounter Books.

Longman, Jere. (2000) *The Girls of Summer: The US Soccer Team and How It Changed the World*. New York. Harper Collins.

Mink, Patsy T., 1927-2002. Patsy T. Mink papers, 1883-2005 (bulk 1953-2002). (2007) Library of Congress, Washington, DC. 880,600 items. 2,638 containers plus 71 oversize

Moss, Marissa. (2013) *Barbed Wire Baseball*. New York. Abrams. Grades 3-5.

National Coalition for Women and Girls in Education. (2002) Report Card on Gender Equity: Title IX at 30. Washington, DC.

Obama, Barack. (2012) "President Barack Obama Reflects on the Impact of Title IX." New York. *Newsweek*. 6/24/12.

Sinnott, Susan. (2003) *Extraordinary Asian Americans and Pacific Islanders: Extraordinary People*. Danbury, CT. Children's Press. Grades 4-6.

Uchida, Yoshiko. (1996) *The Bracelet*. New York. Puffin Books. Grades 2-5.

Yamasaki, Katie. (2013) *Fish For Jimmy*. New York. Holiday House. Grades 2-5

WEBSITES

https://www.loc.gov/rr/mss/mink/mink-about.html

http://history.house.gov/Exhibition-and-Publications/WIC/Women-in-Congress/

http://www.titleix.info/history/the-living-law.aspx

AMAZING ASIAN AMERICANS

Amazing Asian Americans,
a series for the elementary school child.

Reading level 4th—5th grade
Interest level 3rd grade and up

Books in this series:
Vera Wang, Queen of Fashion

Yo-Yo and Yeou-Cheng Ma, Finding Their Way

Astronaut Kalpana Chawla, Reaching for the Stars

To purchase copies visit our website:
dragoneagle.com